ABSTRACT

OF A

NEW METHOD

TO

ANALYZE

The English Language and Literature.

ENGLISH,

THE YOUNGEST, MOST ELASTIC, AND GRAMMATICALLY THE SIMPLEST LANGUAGE. ITS ORIGIN AND PROGRESS PHILOLOGICALLY, HISTORICALLY, AND NUMERICALLY PROVED. ITS INFLUENCE AND IMPORTANCE AS A MEANS OF CIVILIZATION. ITS EXTENT AND DESTINY.

BY

John A. Weisse, M.D.

"Language is an art, and a glorious one, whose influence extends over all others, and in which all science whatever must centre; but an art springing from necessity, and originally invented by artless men."

HORNE TOOKE'S "*Diversions of Purley.*" Vol. I. p. 317. L. E.

NEW-YORK:

PRINTED BY H. LUDWIG, 39 CENTRE-STREET.

1873.

CHAPTER I.

INTRODUCTORY.

Epitome of the Progress of the English Language; its Advantages over other Tongues; its Drawbacks.

In Sharon Turner's "History of the Anglo-Saxons," we read: "To explore the history of any language is a task peculiarly difficult at this period of the world, in which we are so remote from the era of its construction. We have as yet witnessed no people in the act of forming their language, and cannot therefore from experience demonstrate the simple elements, from which a language begins, nor the additional organization, which it gradually receives."

We assent to this statement, when applied to any of the ancient idioms, as: Aryan, Sanscrit, Chaldee, Zend, Hebrew, Arabic, Phœnician, Coptic, Etruscan, Celtic, Basque, Greek, Latin, Gothic, German, Sclavonic, &c.; but English, being the latest linguistic offspring, we shall endeavor to show its "*simple elements*," and to trace "*the additional organization*, which *it gradually receives*". To perform this "*task peculiarly difficult at this period of the world*," we ask and answer the following questions:

I. What is the origin of the English language from A. D. 1600 to our times?

II. What was the language in England from Ethelbert, King of Kent, A. D. 570, to Edward the Confessor, A. D. 1043, and William the Conqueror, A. D. 1066?

III. What was its progress from William the Conqueror, A. D. 1066, to A. D. 1400, when Chaucer, the pioneer of English literature, died?

IV. What was its progress from Chaucer, A. D. 1400, to Shakespeare, A. D. 1600?

V. What is its present extent, importance, and influence as a means of civilization?

VI. What is its Destiny?

To answer these questions we select Anglo-Saxon, English

and American writers of different styles and on different subjects, take extracts, arrange the words under appropriate headings, and arrive at numeric results. Again from these tables of 100 words each we drop repetitions, choose the different nouns, verbs, adjectives, adverbs of quality, and particles, place them in separate columns, and thus reach ultimate totals, which must irrevocably settle the origin and progress of the English language. Poetry, prose, the pulpit, the Forum, the university, the Press, School- and lecture-room, and the fireside furnish their quota to this analysis.

We are convinced there are thousands, who desire satisfactory answers to the above questions, language being a nation's intellectual and moral mirror. To those, who sincerely seek knowledge, we present tables and columns of Anglo-Saxon and English words; to those, who, from prejudice, ignorance, or want of proper research, parade the terms "*Anglo-Saxon, Teutonic, Norman, or Norman-French*, and think they have exhausted the subject, we offer linguistic transitions with percentages. We thought long and earnestly, till we reached this new Method of analyzing the English language and literature. If it affords as much pleasure to readers as it did to the author, who, at the age of thirty knew not a word of English, his labor of thirty years will be amply rewarded. He offers it to the English-speaking populations as a linguistic monument to supply an educational want, hoping it will find its way into schools, colleges and universities.

In this numeric investigation from Ethelbert's Anglo-Saxon Code, A. D. 597 to Milton's "Paradise Lost" 1670, we found this curious linguistic progression:

From A. D. 600 to 900 the dialect was pure Anglo-Saxon.
" 900 to 1100 we find 6 per-cent Græco-Latin.
" 1100 " 1200 " 14 " " "
" 1200 " 1300 " 16 " " "
" 1300 " 1400 " 33 " " "
" 1400 " 1500 " 33 " " "
" 1500 " 1600 " 32 " " "
" 1600 " 1670 " 35 " " "
" 1670 " 1870 Græco-Latin rose to 62 per-cent in some authors.

This progressive influx of words from a different and more advanced family of languages and dialects, unconformable to the Anglo-Saxon Grammar, compelled a relinquishment of odd inflexions. Aimless and arbitrary declension, conjugation and construction were simplified, shortened and generalized to suit from 6 to 62 new comers. Here was the knell of Anglo-Saxon stagnation and the dawn of English progress. The great linguist, Jacob Grimm, consoles Anglo-Saxon enthusiasts by assuring them, that modern English gained in spiritual maturity, what it may have lost in Anglo-Saxon inflexions. The ultimate result of our strict analysis shows over two-thirds of Græco-Latin, and less than one-third of Anglo-Saxon or Gotho-Germanic. After all, language is the truest gauge of a nation's advancement.

No doubt, Shakespeare and Milton settled the character of the English idiom from about 1600 to 1670. From our analysis of the Anglo-Saxon dialect through its transition into the present composite English language we infer, that Ethelbert of A. D. 600 could hardly have conversed with Ethelred II., A. D. 1000; that Egbert of A. D. 828 could not have easily read Chaucer's "*Canterbury Tales*" of 1380; and should Alfred the Great suddenly appear at queen Victoria's Court and address Her Majesty in the Anglo Saxon of A. D. 900, some linguist would be called to interpret the distinguished Stranger's idiom. Hence Sir Charles Lyell's saying: "None of the tongues now spoken, were in existence ten centuries ago," is literally true.

The changes of the Anglo-Saxon dialect from Ethelbert, A. D. 597, to Chaucer 1370, were striking; from Chaucer, 1370, to Shakespeare 1600, they were less so; and from 1600 to our day, they were comparatively slight, as may be realized by our tables. Shakespeare, with his varied conceptions, did not burst the mould of England's dialect; for some admirer counted the words in his writings and states them to be 15,000; probably Mrs. Cowden Clarke, who made a concordance of Shakespeare's works. Milton did not beggar his native tongue, for he only employs 8,000. The translation of the Scriptures, under James I., 1611, did not exhaust it, although it required 773,746 words, of which about 98/100 are proper names and repetitions, if it be true, that the insignificant particle ***and*** occurs 46,219 times. No doubt, these figures were taken from concordances. It is said few good authors use 10,000 words, while ordinary people employ but 3000, which is but a fraction of the 80,000 *popular*, *scientific*, *and technical* words, mentioned in Noah Webster's preface to his dictionary of 1840, in which he says: "It has been my aim in this work—to furnish a standard of our vernacular tongue, which we shall not be ashamed to bequeath to *five hundred millions of people*, who are destined to occupy, and hope to adorn, the vast territory within our jurisdiction." Since then Texas, California and Alaska were added. Trench, in his "Study of Words," corroborates the superiority of language over authors in this felicitous strain: "Far more and mightier in every way is a language than any one of the works which may have been composed in it; for that work, great as it may be, is but the embodying of the mind of a single man, this of a nation. The *Iliad* is great, yet not so great in strength or power or beauty as the Greek language. "*Paradise Lost*" is a noble possession for a people to have inherited, but the English tongue is a nobler heritage yet."

English, now the easiest language as to grammar, combining the elegance of the Græco-Latin with the vigor of the Gotho-Germanic tongues, would be ready for *universal adoption*, if the English-speaking peoples would adopt the plain phonographic German rule: *Write as you pronounce, and pronounce as you write;* in other words: write the same letter or letters for one sound, wherever that sound is required, and utter the same sound for the same letter or letters, wherever you find the letter or letters. This same plain phonographic German rule has been applied over two thousand years to Greek and Latin, not only by the nations of continental Europe, but of Asia, Africa, and South America.— A Greek or Latin scholar of France, Germany, Italy, Spain, Scandinavia, Russia, Siberia, or even Turkey can converse in these classic languages with a scholar of Arabia, Armenia, Persia, Tartary, Egypt, Morocco, Brazil, Peruvia, or Mexico, because among all those heterogeneous and distant nations *Greek and Latin are written as they are pronounced and pronounced as they are written.* Strange, the Isle of Britain and North America should stand in their own light and attempt to carry their inconsistent pronunciation into those classic idioms, which ought to be a sacred universal linguistic medium for the educated of all climes, whether from Oxford, Heidelberg, Mecca, Fez, Yale, or Rio Janeiro. This so-called English pronunciation of Greek and Latin has not as yet obtained even in Ireland, where a classic student from any part of the world, except Oxford and Yale, can attend divine service and understand every word uttered by the officiating priest; so can any classic scholar attend and understand mass in the Convent of Mount St. Bernard or of Mount Carmel. Is it not high time the English and Americans should awake, not only from their night-mare pronunciation of Greek and Latin, but from the nightmare phonography of their own superior language, whose *universal adoption* is thereby retarded? We are told, the German phonographic rule would be impossible in English. If it has been possible for centuries in German, Greek and Latin, why should it be impossible in English or any other language? To pronounce the same letter or letters differently in certain words or in one and the same word, seems not only strange but capricious to unbiassed observers. Such is the case with *ou* in *flour*, *four*, *hour*, *pour*, &c. with *ough* in *bough*, *cough*, *dough*, &c. with *ow* in *bow*, n. and v., *row*, n. and v., *sow*, n. and v., &c. We might multiply such anomalies, but let these suffice here and now, we shall give more details and suggest a remedy in our chapter on orthoëpy and phonography. English-speaking people do not seem to notice these irregularities. To tax the memories of their own children with linguistic conundrums, is not only wrong, but cruel. Of all sciences, language should be made as simple and easy as possible; for man's labors are so numerous and varied, that it is useless to waste his time in minutiæ of spelling-books and "*Pronouncing-Dictionaries*," where at the top of each page, are guide-words with numbered vowels, and where each word in the text is printed doubly and differently to indicate its pronunciation. Foreigners, who have studied and realized the advantages of the English idiom, as to grammar and construction, regret that the English and Americans, so eminently practical in other matters, continue to tolerate such glaring inconsistency in their language, a faculty, science and art, which they must use daily and hourly from the moment they rise till they retire. Yet, by a concerted effort to write and print as they pronounce, and pronounce as they write and print, this arbitrariness might be removed from their language, if not in a year, at most in half a century. To say nothing of the many useless letters, dropped by such a course, the time saved in type-setting, the ink and paper economized, just consider, how simple, easy and consistent the English language would be! Why, a bright child of seven could master it in one year; an intelligent adult in two years; a scholar in six months. Surely, if this improvement is not made now, when there are but one hundred millions of English-speaking people, can it be made with more hope of success, when there will be five hundred millions? In his "Intellectual Life" Hamerton observes: "A language cannot be thoroughly learned by an adult without five years' residence in the country where it is spoken; and without habits of close observation, a residence of twenty years is insufficient." Alas, this is too true, not only with regard to English, but with regard to other languages, past and present! will it be so with language to come? Let the English-speaking populations once realize, how easy the acquisition of their tongue would be for their own children and foreigners, if the same letter or letters were strictly adapted to one sound, and one sound to the same letter or letters; then no intelligent Englishman or Yankee would rest, until anomalies and irregularities would be removed from their language, now the admiration of philologists, as may be seen by our quotations.

It is said 100 students are employed at Jeddo to simplify the Japanese characters so as to adapt them to the sounds of the European languages. If a nation, that was but yesterday considered barbarous, is acting thus, why should not England and America call a scientific convention to harmonize the letters of their alphabet with the sounds of their language? Why should not all the modern nations have a philologic congress to extend into language the uniformity we have in mathematics, chemistry, and music? The Arabic figures, algebraic characters, and mathematical signs have been and are used and understood at sight, not only by Arabs, Turks, English, French, Germans, Italians, Spaniards, and Scandinavians, but by Russians; so are Lavoisier's chemical symbols and equivalents. Notes and musical language are read and played at sight by artists of all nations, not only from one and the same composer, but from one and the same sheet. Why not have such uniformity and unanimity as to sounds, signs, and characters in language, in which, according to Horne Tooke, "*all science whatever must centre?*"

As to the destiny of the English language, the myriads, who speak it in Europe, America, Asia, Africa and Oceanica, are fully aware of its capacity to become the universal linguistic medium, which may be realized by looking at the map of North America, where the English idiom has, within twenty-five years, spread from the Atlantic and Gulf of Mexico to the Pacific and Behring's straits, and displaced the Spanish, Indian, and Russian dialects. Cuba, St. Domingo, Mexico, Central America, the Sandwich and Navigators' Islands are feeling its influence and desire its sway; even exclusive China and Japan seem to lean more and more towards America and the English language across the Pacific. Thus the tide of empire is not only westward, but eastward; it meets and mingles in America.

In his "Lectures on the English Language," p. 121, G. P Marsh says: "In order to arrive at satisfactory conclusions on this point (*origin of the English language*), more thorough and extensive research is necessary." In our extracts and tables the "*more thorough and extensive research,*" urged by Mr. Marsh, will be found. There we even supply the want, felt by the erudite lecturer, when he says, p. 122: "I have made no attempt to assign words, not of Anglo-Saxon origin, to their respective sources." We made the attempt and found, that the respective sources of the English vocabulary are: *Anglo-Saxon, Gothic, Danish, Swedish, German, Dutch, and Icelandic; Welsh, Scotch, Irish, and Armoric; Greek, Latin, French, Italian, Spanish, and Portuguese; Hebrew and Arabic; and Russian.* Hence a careful perusal of this analysis will enable any reader to learn, that the English of to-day is a compound of twenty idioms, ancient and modern, dead and living. No wonder Wilberforce says: "English is a composite language." To realize that England's dialect has added from 6 to 62 per-cent of

Græco-Latin since Alfred the Great, must prove interesting to the English-speaking millions over all the globe.

Our extracts and tables show these curious facts: 1st, teachers, professors, and grammarians abound in *repetitions;* next come journalists, preachers, political speakers, lecturers, scientists and historians; last, but not least, poets, whom measure and rhyme compel to be Laconic. 2d. More than half the words, even in the works of the best English authors, are *particles.* * If such is the case in print, what shall be said of daily intercourse and conversation? It is to be hoped telegraphing, phonography and philology will do away with linguistic prolixity, in order to save time, ink and paper, to say nothing of vocal organs. Spartan Laconism in speech and print and Pythagorian schools would not come amiss in this age of small print and smaller talk. Less tongue, more brain; fewer words, more thought; less grammar, less syntax, more practice; less preaching, more example, would soon lead towards a higher intellectual, moral and social standard. All tends to shorten space by air-line Rail Roads, time by telegraphs, labor by machinery. This is well; but why not carry this tendency into language? Certain styles of writing demand more or less Anglo-Saxon, while others require more or less Græco-Latin: for domestic subjects Anglo-Saxon almost suffices; whereas topics of science, art and progress require Græco-Latin. Thus one and the same author, writing a poem on domestic affairs unconsciously uses 80 per-cent Anglo-Saxon and 20 per-cent Græco-Latin, yet in the preface he uses but 60 per-cent Anglo-Saxon and 40 per-cent Græco-Latin. The only reason we can assign for this is, that the one is primitive, the other progressive.

Of all sciences the sublimest — language — is the most complicated and inconsistent, not for want of votaries, but for want of strictly scientific analysis and synthesis. In our tables, let the reader compare the words of the Græco-Latin and the Anglo-Saxon columns and realize, that nearly all the Græco-Latin, are words of progress, civilization and refine-

---

* Articles, prepositions, conjunctions, interjections, and most adverbs of place and time, we call *particles*, or words without inherent meaning; while we style nouns, verbs, adjectives, and adverbs, formed from adjectives, *words with inherent meaning.*

ment, whereas almost one-half of the Anglo-Saxon are insignificant particles and words of primary necessity. According to Tyrwhit's "Essay on the Language and Versification of Chaucer," p. 7, the French element, in the Anglo-Saxon dialect, began with the accession of Edward the Confessor, (1043); and not, as usually asserted, with the so-called Norman Conquest, which but hastened the fusion of the two idioms. In this analysis we fully realize what Mr. Marsh says p. 122: "Words of original Latin etymology have been, in the great majority of instances, borrowed from the French and are still used in forms more in accordance with the French than with the Latin orthography." No wonder, the English under Edward the Confessor ceased to cultivate Anglo-Saxon and introduced French. Swinton's adage: "When a tongue becomes petrified the national mind walks out of it," was fully realized under Hardicanute. The Anglo-Saxon dialect was too poor and contracted for an Anglo-French population, who mixed the two idioms in such proportions as suited their progress in morals, literature, science, art, commerce and civilization. As they progressed from Egbert to Victoria, their language advanced towards its present standard of excellence.

The English character is a happy mixture of Celtic wit, Franco-Norman daring, and Germanic gravity, tinged with a peculiar love of enterprize and distant adventure. Perhaps the varied tribal and national elements, that engendered the English, together with their hazy island-home, tended to produce a race distinguished for sagacious ecclecticism, not only in science, art, mechanics and manufactures, but in language.

In this numeric analysis of the English language, we realize the workings of the English and American mind; its power to expand, accrete and excrete; its faculty to select and assimilate; its versatility and progress in literature, science, art, mechanics and manufactures. The English idiom is the cream and essence of the Aryo-European dialects: it contains the choicest Græco-Latin, Gotho-Germanic and Celtic elements: A happy medium between French and German; more grave than the former; less guttural, harsh, inverted and cumbersome than the latter; grammatically simpler than either; but very capricious in its orthoëpy and phonography, which might be easily modified. Vowels and consonants are so felicitously combined in the English language, that the dwellers of the frigid and torrid zones can articulate and speak it with comparative ease. No wonder, Dr. Rapp says: "The nations of Europe may esteem themselves fortunate, that the English have not made the discovery of the suitableness of their language for universal adoption." Our numeric investigation also shows, that the English language improved in Laconism and directness, as it progressed from Ethelbert, 597, to Victoria, 1873: Less words and fewer particles are almost the rule.

"*The whole Earth was of one language and of one speech.*" Such is the declaration of Moses, Gen. XI, 1. Hence we realize his appreciation of language thirty-five centuries ago. Much has been said and written as to the origin, character and name of that one language and one speech, so emphatically mentioned in the oldest known Record. There can be little doubt as to the one language hereafter; for already the sun never sets on the English-speaking populations; already the Oceans, seas, and isles resound with English. Hence travel, Englishmen; travel, Americans; already not only the Esquimaux and Ethiopian, but the American Indian, Australian, and Hindoo speak English; already hotel-waiters in Europe have to pass a competitive examination in the English language; spend your gold! By so doing, you diffuse and expand your language, and with it your influence and civilization. Should the author of this work contribute one iota towards a universal language, he would consider his Earth-life as a link in the endless chain of progression. As he claims Saxon origin and traces his ancestry to the Fatherland, this book can hardly be considered partial. Impartiality is his aim, truth his object. No doubt, the English language with the Decimal System of measures, weights, and moneys, as a means of intercourse, would simplify commerce, facilitate travel, and favor universal education. They would be the crowning glory to printing, steam, and telegraph. National boundaries, jealousies, custom-houses and all manner of prejudice would vanish like mist before a genial sun. The English Sovereign and President of the United States, who initiate this movement, will figure in History as the greatest benefactors of mankind. We hope the international Congress, about to meet in Paris, July 22, 1873, after discussing the Japanese and other Asiatic idioms, will find time to direct attention towards the language, that is simplest in its alphabet, grammar, and construction, and choicest in its vocabulary; then call for an international congress of linguists to consider its *universal adoption.* If that congress is impartial, they will find English most suitable.

Before we close this Introductory survey of the English-speaking millions, and begin our curious analysis of their language and literature, let us cite a passage from that most erudite living philologist, Max Müller, who preferred his professorship at Oxford to that recently offered him by the Kaiser: "Why certain words die, and others live on, why certain meanings of words become prominent, so as to cause the absorption of all the other meanings, we have no chance to explain. We must take the work of language as we find it, and in disentangling the curious skein, we must not expect to find one continuous thread, but rest satisfied, if we can separate the broken ends, and place them side by side in something like an intelligible order." We shall now endeavor to disentangle the curious skein of the English language, and unroll it in one continuous thread, without separating or replacing any broken ends.

CHAPTER II.

"Θνομα ἂρα διδασκαλικον τί εστιν ὃργανον και διακριτικον τῆς ὐσίας, ὥσπερ κερκὶς ὐφὰστος."—Plato's Cratylus.

Noah Webster, in his "Dictionary of the English Language" of 1861, Author's Preface, p. XIV., says: "What individual is competent to trace to their source, and define in all their various applications, popular, scientific, and technical, *seventy* or *eighty thousand* words!"

We averaged the words therein and found about:

55,524	Græco-Latin	words
22,220	Gotho-Germanic (mostly Anglo-Saxon)	"
443	Celtic	"
98	Sclavonic	"
1,724	Semitic (Hebrew and Arab.)	"
80,011		

We also averaged Walker's "Critical Pronouncing Dictionary and Expositor of the English Language," Edinburgh edition of 1852, and realized about:

56,108	Græco Latin	words.
21,777	Gotho-Germanic (mostly Anglo-Saxon)	"
461	Celtic	"
768	Semitic	"
79,114		

These figures from Webster's and Walker's Dictionaries show *nearly three-quarters of Græco-Latin, and about one-quarter of Anglo-Saxon.*

Thomas Shaw, in his "Outlines of English Literature," p. 44, says: "The English now consists of about 38,000 words." Some anonymous writer, who had the patience to count the words in each part of speech, observes: "There are in the English language 20,500 nouns; 40 pronouns; 9,200 adjectives; 8,000 verbs; 2,600 adverbs; 69 prepositions; 19 conjunctions; 68 interjections; and 2 articles; in all about 40,498 words." No doubt, the figures of Shaw and of the anonymous writer, refer to school-dictionaries, in which many scientific and technical words are omitted. Since people speak of language, as though it were within the covers of some Dictionary or Encyclopedia, let us survey its domain as to time, space, and importance: according to the Sacred Record language antidates everything, even light; for God said: Let there be light, called the light *Day*, the darkness *Night*, the firmament *Heaven*, the gathering together of the waters *Seas*, &c. . . . . (Gen. I, 3—11.) Thus Elohim uttered and formed language, before He made man, animals, or plants. Language embraces Zoölogy and the names of its 245,000 living species of animals; Botany and the names of its 100,000 living species of plants; Geology with its 95,000 fossil species of animals and 2500 fossil species of plants; Mineralogy with its myriads of crystals, metals and minerals. Language includes, not only, the ordinary dictionary of 40,000 popular words, but the Classical Lexicon, the Dictionaries of Medicine, Jurisprudence, Chemistry, Arts and Manufactures, Biography, and the universal Gazetteer. The 4000 Christian names, the Bible names and the innumerable family names, also belong to language. Have we not compassed language? Not yet: Look at yonder cathedral and churches with their lofty spires; at those grand edifices, reared for parliaments, congresses, legislatures, courts, institutes, universities, faculties, colleges, theatres; watch that post-office and the mails streaming to and from it; glance at those newspaper palaces, issuing bulletins and extras; behold those wires, freighted with the tersest and choicest treasures of language, rapping out telegrams in yonder office; see those structures, erected for casting type, printing, binding, publishing, and selling books. Forget not the 84 Bible societies and agencies, that issued and distributed 110,000,000 Bibles and Testaments since 1804—one and all were founded to diffuse and convey thought by and through language, either spoken, written, printed, or mapped. Should the God, who originated language on Earth, strike mankind dumb to-day, to-morrow these architectural splendors would begin to fade, for language raised them; language underlies them all. Now we can exclaim with Horne Tooke: "Language is an art and a glorious one, whose influence extends over all others, and in which all science whatever must centre." Hence should not this most powerful of engines—*language*—be made as simple, easy, fluent, and perfect as possible? Lift your eyes to that azured dome! When you have learned, that language gave names and lent speech to those comets, moons, planets, suns, stars, constellations, and galaxies, you will be able to realize Jean Paul Richter's striking simile on language:

„Mich dünkt, der Mensch würde sich, (so wie das sprachlose Thier, das in der äußeren Welt, wie in einem dunkeln, betäubenden Wellen-Meere schwimmt), ebenfalls in dem vollgestirnten Himmel der äußeren Anschauung dumpf verlieren, wenn er das verworrene Leuchten nicht durch Sprache in Sternbilder abtheilte, und sich durch diese das Ganze in Theile für das Bewußtsein auflösete."

From this survey of language's vast domain we conclude, that the *English Vocabulary* should number, at least, *one million of words* to satisfy present science, art, and literature. No wonder then, the German Universal Dictionary, now issuing by the Brothers Grimm, is to contain 500,000 words!

CHAPTER III.

Anglo-Saxon Extracts from A. D. 597 to A. D. 900.

Code of Ethelbert, King of Kent, A. D. 597.

ANGLO-SAXON.*

"Gif Cyning his leode to him gehatath, and heom mon thaer yfel gedo, II. bote and cyning L. scillinga.

Gif in Cyninges tune man mannan ofsleah, L. scillinga gebete.

Gif on Eorles tune man mannan ofsleath, XII. scillinga gebete.

Gif man thone man ofsleahth. XX. scillinga gebete.

Gif thuman (of a slaehth), XX. scillinga. Gif thuman naegl of weordeth III. scillinga gebete. Gif man scyte-finger (of a slaehth), VIII. scillinga gebete Gif man middle-finger (of a slaehth), IV. scillinga gebete. Gif man gold-finger (of a slaehth), VI. scillinga gebete. Gif man thon litlan finger (of a slaehth), XI. scillinga gebete."

ENGLISH.

"If King his people to him calls, and any one there evil does, two fines shall be paid, and to the King fifty shillings.

If in the King's town a man slay a man, fifty shillings shall be paid.

If in an Earl's town a man slay a man, twelve shillings shall be paid.

If a man slay any man, twenty shillings shall be paid.

If the thumb be cut off, twenty shillings. If the thumb nail be cut off, three shillings shall be paid. If a man cut off the forefinger, eight shillings shall be paid. If a man cut off the middle finger, four shillings shall be paid. If a man cut off the gold (ring) finger, six shillings shall be paid. If any man cut off the little finger, eleven shillings shall be paid."

Saxon Chronicle, A. D., 891.

"An. DCCCXCI. Her for se here east, and Earnulf cyning gefeaht with thaem raede-here aer tha scipu comon, mid East-Francum, and Seaxum, and Baegerum, and hine geflymde. And thry Scottas cwomon to Aelfrede cyninge on anum bate, butan aelcum gerethum of Hibernia; and thonon hi woldon for Godes lufan on eltheodinesse bion, hy ne rohton hwaer.

Se bat waes geworht of thriddan healfre hyde, the hie on foron, and hi namon mid him that hie haefdon to seofon nihtum mete, and tha comon hie ymb seofon niht, to londe on Cornwealum, and foran tha sona to Aelfrede cyninge."

"An. 891. Here fared the army east, and King Earnulf fought with the riding army (cavalry) ere the ships came with the East-Francs. and Saxons and Bavarians, and defeated them. And three Scots came to King Alfred in a boat, without any rowers, from Hibernia; and thence they departed, because they would for God's love be in a state of pilgrimage, they did not care where.

The boat was made of three hides and a half, in which they fared. and they took with them that they had for seven nights meat. and they came about the seventh night, to land in Cornwall, and fared to King Alfred."

Anglo-Saxon Version of Orosius by King Alfred A. D., 900.

"Ohthere saede his hlaforde, Aelfrede kyninge, thaet he ealra North-man, north mest bude. He cwaeth that he bude on thaem lande north-weardum with tha west sae. He saede theah thaet landsy swythe north thanon; ac hit is eall west but on feavum slowum sticce maelum wiciath Finnas."

"Ohthere said to his lord, King Alfred, that he lived northmost of all the north-men He quoth that he dwelled in the land northward with the west sea. He said, though that land is quite north from thence; and it is all waste but in a few places, where for the most part dwell the Finns."†

In the above extracts are 237 common words, of *which* 108 *are particles.*

* We give these extracts in the Roman character because, as Sir David Dalrymple pertinently observes: "The uncouthness of the Anglo-Saxon character deters many from examining what they would understand, if they could read."

† Sinding in his "*History of Scandinavia,*" p. 20, says: "On the entrance of the Goths into Scandinavia, the land was inhabited by two reciprocally kindred nations, whose present names are Laplanders and Finns."

Origin of 100 different Words from the preceding Extracts of Ethelbert's Code, A. D. 597, Saxon Chronicle, A. D. 891, and Anglo-Saxon Version of Orosius by Alfred the Great, A. D. 900.

Aryo*—European Type of Languages:									Aryo-Phoenician Type:
PELEGO-PELASGIC OR GRÆCO-LATIN FAMILY.		GOTHO-GERMANIC FAMILY:				GOMERO-CELTIC FAMILY.	SCLAVONIC FAMILY.		SEMITIC FAMILY.
Greek:	**French:**	**Anglo-Saxon:**							
		Gif	slaehth	butan	mete				
		Cyning	naegl	aelcum	ymb				
		his	weordeth	gerethum	night				
		leode	scyte-finger	hi	londe				
		to	middle	betaelon	sona				**Result:**
		gehatath	gold	forthon	saede				100 Anglo-Saxon.†
		and	litlan	the	hlaforde				
Latin:		heom	Her	woldon	ealra				
		mon	for	Godes	North				
		thaer	se	lufan	mest				
		yfel	here	eltheodinesse	bude				
		gedo	east	bion	cwaeth				
		bote	gefeaht	ne	west				
		scillinga	with	rohton	sae				
		in	thaem	geworht	theah				
		tune	raede	thriddan	swythe				
		man	aer	healfre	ac				
		ofsleah	tha	hyde	hit				
		gebete	scipu	hie	eall				
		on	comon	foron	buton				
		Eorles	hine	namon	feawum				
		thone	geflymde	that	stowum				
		thuman	thry	heafdon	sticce				
		of	anum	seofon	mealum				
		a	bate	nihtum	wiciath				
Græco-Latin Words:		**Anglo-Saxon Words:** 100, of which 31 are particles.				**Celtic:**	**Sclavonic:**		**Semitic:**

* The above classification is based on modern and ancient linguistic investigations: *Aryo* from Max Müller's *Aryan*, which has recently been considered the primitive dialect. *Pelego*, from *Peleg*, Gen. X., 25; *Pelasgic*, from *Pelasgi*, Herodotus lib. I., LVII.; *Gomero*, from *Gomer*, Gen. X., 2; and *Semitic*, from *Shem*, (Sem) Gen. V., 32, which has been generally adopted in Philology for this family of languages.

† Hence we realize, that: "The language, spoken in England before the Norman invasion, had been for some centuries a pure Saxon dialect, unmixed with Latin or British." Petrit Andrews' "*History of Great Britain*," Vol. I p. 261., L. E. Perhaps *Anglo-Saxon* instead of Saxon, would have been more appropriate, because the Angles, and not the Saxons, gave their name to the country.

Extract from Chaucer's* "Canterbury Tales,"† A. D. 1400.

Appleton's Edition 1857, p. 578.

"Now have I told you of *veray confession*, that is the *seconde part of* "*penitence*. The thridde *part* is *satisfaction*, and that stont most *generally* "in *almesse* dede and in bodily *peine*. Now ben ther three *maner* of *al-* "*messe: contrition* of herte, wher a man *offreth* himself to God: another "is, to have *pitee* of the *defaute* of his neighbour: and the thridde is, in "yeving of good *conseil*,‡ gostly and bodily, wher as men have nede, and "namely in *sustenance* of mannes food. And take kepe that a man hath "nede of thise thinges *generally*, he hath nede of food, of clothing, and of "herberow, he hath nede of *charitable conseilling* and *visiting* in *prison* and "in *maladie*, and *sepulture* of his ded body. And if thou maiest not *visite* "the nedeful in *prison* in thy *person*, *visite* hem with thy *message*, and "thy yeftes. Thise ben *generally* the *almesses* and werkes of *charitee*, of "hem that have *temporel richesses*, or *discretion* in *conseilling*. Of thise "werkes§ shalt thou heren at the day of dome."

"This *almesse* shuldest thou do of thy *propre* thinges, and *hastily*, and "*prively* if thou maiest: but natheles, if thou mayest not do it *prively*, thou "shalt not forbere to do *almesse*, though men see it, so that it be not don "for thanke of the world, but only to have thanke of Jesu *Crist*. For as "witnesseth Seint Mathewe, Cap. &c."

229 common words, among which

The	occurs	7	times.			65	
a	"	2	"	be (aux.)	occurs	5	times.
of	"	20	"	have (aux.)	"	8	"
to	"	4	"	shall	"	3	"
from	"	0	"	will (aux.)	"	0	"
in	"	9	"	may	"	2	"
with	"	1	"	do (aux.)	"	0	"
by	"	0	"	that	"	5	"
Pron. of 1st person		1	"	and	"	15	"
" 2d "		11	"				
" 3d "		10	"			103	
				other particles		33	
		65					
						133 particles.	

* "To penetrate the mists, which balefully lowered over the English tongue, the brightness of a Chaucer, the accuracy of a Gower were needed, and those constellations were not yet visible." Pettit Andrews' "History of Great Britain."

† Marsh (Lectures on the English language, p 124) says: "Chaucer uses 80 per-cent Anglo-Saxon. Our analysis shows but 63 per-cent, 30 of which are mere particles. Hence there are nearly as many French as Anglo-Saxon words of inherent meaning in Chaucer's style.

‡ 18 of the 31 French words printed in Italics, in the Table, are now spelt in French, as when Chaucer introduced them into English from 1360 to 1400.

§ *Werkes* is the present German for *work*.

Origin 100 different words from the preceding Extract of Chaucer's Canterbury Tales, A. D. 1400.

Aryo—European Type of Languages:

PELEGO-PELASGIC OR GRÆCO-LATIN FAMILY:				GOTHO-GERMANIC FAMILY:				GOMERO-CELTIC FAMILY.	SCLAVONIC FAMILY:	ARYO PHOENICIAN TYPE: SEMITIC FAMILY:
Greek:	**Latin**:	**French**:		**Anglo-Saxon**.			**German**:			
	veray.	*Confesssion*	*temporel*	Now	to	yeftes, n.	as			
	Cap.	*seconde*, adj.	*richesses*	have, aux.	God	or	werkes,◊			
	2	*part*, n.	*discretion*	I	another	shalt, aux.	so			
		penitence	*propre*	told	neighbour	heren, v.	3			
		satisfaction	hastily	you	yeving, v.	day				
		generally	prively	of	good	dome, n.	**Gothic**:			
		almesse, n.	seint, adj.	that	gostly	do				
		peine, n.	citee, n.	is	nede, n.	but, c.	at			
		maner, n.	31‡	the	namely	notheles	1			
		contrition		thridde	food	forbere, v.				
		offreth		and	take	though				
		pitee, n.		stont, v.	kepe, v.	see				
		defaute, n.		most	thise, pro.	for				
		conseil, n.		in	thinges	thanke, n.				
		sustenance		dede, n.	clothing, n.	world				
		charitable		bodily	herberow, n.	only, adv.				
		prison		there	ded, adj.	witnesses, v.				
		maladie		three	if	63†				
		sepulture		herte, n.	thou					
		visite. v.		wher, adv.	maiest, aux.					
		person		a	not					
		message		man. n.	nedeful, n.					
		charitee		himself	with					
Graeco-Latin Words: 33				**Germanic Words**: 67, of which 30 are particles.						

Result:

Latin:	2
French:	31
Anglo-Saxon:	63
German:	3
Gothic:	1
	100

33 per-cent. Græco-Latin.
67 " Germanic.

NOTE: 32 of the 33 Græco Latin words have each an inherent meaning; whereas 30 of the 67 Germanic are mere particles. Hence we infer that Chaucer used 37 per-cent. Germanic and 32 per-cent. Græco-Latin words of inherent meaning; and 31 per-cent. particles.

Extract from Queen Victoria's Speech in Parliament, February 6th, 1866.

MY LORDS AND GENTLEMEN,

"It is with great satisfaction that I have recourse to your asssis-"tance and advice.

"I have recently declared my consent to a marriage between "my daughter, Princess Helena and Prince Christian of Schleswig "Holstein Sonderbourg-Augustenburg. I trust this union may be "prosperous and happy.

"The death of my beloved uncle, the King of the Belgians, has "affected me with profound grief. I feel great confidence, however, "that the wisdom, which he evinced during his reign, will animate "his successor, and preserve for Belgium her independence and "prosperity.

"My relations with foreign powers are friendly and satisfactory, "and I see no cause to fear any disturbance of the general peace.

"The meeting of the fleets of France and England in the ports "of the respective countries has tended to cement the amity of the "two nations, and to prove to the world their friendly concert in "the promotion of peace.

"I have observed with satisfaction that the United States, after "terminating successfully the severe struggle in which they were "so long engaged, are wisely repairing the ravages of civil war. "The abolition of slavery is an event calling, &c.

178 common words, among which

The	occurs	17	times.	be	occurs	6	times.
a	"	2	"	have	"	5	"
of	"	11	"	shall	"	0	"
to	"	6	"	will	"	1	"
from	"	0	"	may	"	1	"
in	"	3	"	do	"	0	"
with	"	4	"	that	"	3	"
by	"	0	"	and	"	6	"
Pron. of 1st person		11	"				
" 2d "		1	"			84	
" 3d "		7	"		other particles	11	
						95	particles.

☞ *As every word in a document like this, is considered and studied by the author, and eagerly canvassed by every Englishman, that can read, it is a fit linguistic representative of its day.*

Origin of 100 different words from the preceding Extract of Queen Victoria's Address to Parliament, February 6th, 1866.

Aryo–European Type of Languages:										Aryo-Phoenician Type:
PELEGO-PELASGIC OR GRÆCO-LATIN FAMILY:				GOTHO-GERMANIC FAMILY:				GOMERO CELTIC FAMILY:	SCLAVONIC FAMILY:	SEMITIC FAMILY:
Greek:	**Latin**:	**French**:		**Anglo-Saxon**:		**German**:		**Welsh**:		
	Evinced animate, v. successor disturbance United States terminating slavery event calling, n. 10	satisfaction recourse assistance advice recently declared consent, n. marriage Princess Prince union prosperous uncle affected profound grief confidence during, prep reign, n. preserve independence prosperity relations foreign powers satisfactory cause, n.	general peace parts respective countries tended cement, v. amity nations prove concert promotion observed successfully severe engaged repairing ravages civil abolition 47	It is with great that I have to your a between daughter this may, aux. the death of beloved king feel however wisdom which will, aux. for friendly see	no fear, v. any meeting, n. fleets, n. in two world after long wisely war 39	so 1 **Danish**: trust, v. 1		happy struggle, n. 2		**Result**: Latin: 10 French: 47 Anglo-Saxon: 39 German: 1 Danish: 1 Welsh: 2 100 57 per-cent. Græco-Latin. 41 per-cent. Germanic. 2 per-cent. Celtic.
Graeco-Latin Words: 57.				**Germanic Words**: 41, of which 20 are particles.				**Celtic Words**: 2.		

NOTE: 56 of the 57 Græco-Latin words have each an inherent meaning; whereas 20 of the 41 Germanic are mere particles. Hence we infer, that Queen Victoria uses about 21 per-cent. Germanic and 56 per-cent. Græco-Latin words of inherent meaning; and 21 per-cent. particles.

Extract from President Grant's Inaugural Address, March 4th, 1869.

Citizens of the United States: Your suffrages having elected me to the office of President of the United States, I have, in conformity with the Constitution of our country, taken the oath of office prescribed therein. I have taken this oath without mental reservation, and with the determination to do, to the best of my ability, all that it requires of me.

The responsibilities of the position I feel, but accept them without fear. The office has come to me unsought: I commence its duties untrammelled. I bring to it a conscientious desire and determination to fill it to the best of my ability to the satisfaction of the people. On all leading questions agitating the public mind I will always express my views to Congress, and urge them according to my judgment, and when I think it advisable, will exercise the constitutional privilege of interposing a veto to defeat measures which I oppose. But all laws will be faithfully executed, whether they meet my approval or not.

I shall on all subjects have a policy to recommend, none to enforce, against the will of the people. Laws are to govern all alike—those opposed to as well &c.....

198 common words, among which

The	occurs	17	times.
a	"	3	"
of	"	9	"
to	"	14	"
from	"	0	"
in	"	1	"
with	"	[illegible]	"
by	"	[illegible]	"
Pron. of 1st person		13	"
" 2d "		1	"
" 3d "		8	"

be	occurs	2	times.
have	"	5	"
shall	"	1	"
will	"	3	"
may	"	0	"
do	"	0	"
and	"	4	"
that	"	1	"
		87	
other particles		18	
		105	particles.

☞ *As every word in a document like this, is considered and studied by the author, and eagerly canvassed by every American that can read, it is a fit linguistic representative of its day.*

Origin of 100 different words from the preceding Extract of President Grant's Inaugural Address, March 4th, 1869.

Aryo—European Type of Languages:									ARYO-PHOENICIAN TYPE:
PELEGO-PELASGIC OR GRÆCO-LATIN FAMILY.				GOTHO-GERMANIC FAMILY:			GOMERO-CELTIC FAMILY:	SLAVONIC FAMILY:	SEMITIC FAMILY:
Greek:	**Latin:**	**French:**		**Anglo-Saxon:**		**German:**	**Armoric:**		
	United	Citizens	advisable	of	leading	all	faith		
	States	suffrages	exercise, v.	the	mind. n.	as	1		
	elected	office	constitutional	your	will, aux.	2			
	prescribed	President	privilege	having	when				**Result:**
	agitating	conformity	interposing	me	think				
	express, v.	constitution	defeat, v.	to	always				Latin: 10
	Congress	country	measures, n.	in	which				French: 41
	urge	mental	oppose	with	law				Anglo Saxon: 46
	veto, n.	reservation	executed	taken	be, aux.				German: 2
	subjects, n	determination	approval	oath	fully				Armoric: 1
	10	ability	policy	therein	whether				100
		requires	recommend	this	meet, v.				51 per-cent. Græco-Latin.
		responsibilities	enforce	without	or				48 per-cent. Germanic
		position	govern	and	not				1 per-cent. Celtic.
		accept	41	do	shall				
		commence		best	none				
		duties		that	against				
		unt[illegible], adj		it	alike				
		conscientious		feel	well				
		desire, n.		but	46				
		satisfaction		fear, n.					
		people. n.		come					
		questions, n.		unsought					
		public, adj.		bring					
		views, n.		a					
		according, prep.		fill					
		judgment		on					
Graeco-Latin Words: 51.				**Germanic Words:** 48, of which 28 are particles.			**Celtic Words:** 1.		

NOTE: The 51 Græco-Latin words have each an inherent meaning; whereas 28 of the 48 Germanic are mere particles. Hence we infer, that President Grant uses about 20 per-cent. Germanic and 51 per-cent. Græco-Latin words of inherent meaning; and 28 per-cent. particles.

The ultimate result of this chapter, as to the origin of the different words contained in the tables of 20 English and 20 American authors and writers, is *nearly three-quarters Græco-Latin, and about one-quarter Anglo-Saxon*, which corroborates our averages of Noah Webster's and Walker's dictionaries.

☞ *The object of this work, to which the author has devoted his leisure-hours for thirty years, is:*

I. To lay before the English-speaking populations in both hemispheres the real origin and progress of their Language.

II. To make the coming generation realize the superiority of their idiom over others, as to the refinement and vigor of its vocabulary, clearness of diction, simplicity in grammar, and directness in construction.

III. To show the inconsistency of English orthography.

IV. To suggest a method to write and print English as it is pronounced, and remove the few remaining irregularities from its grammar.

V. Last, but not least, to stimulate the English-speaking millions all over the globe, so to simplify the uttering, writing, and printing of their language, as to make it a desideratum for universal adoption, and do for English what was said 638 *B. C. by Zephaniah III.* 9: *"For then will I turn to the people a pure language, that they may all call upon the name of the Lord, to serve Him with one consent." True, the Prophet spoke of Hebrew—yet let every intelligent Englishman and American say here and now: We will give to the World a language, written as it pronounced and free from grammatic irregularities.*

www.ingramcontent.com/pod-product-compliance
Lightning Source LLC
LaVergne TN
LVHW011142110826
845150LV00008B/2476
* 9 7 8 1 4 1 8 1 9 2 2 2 8 *